MW01716761

14

# HARUN

upon whom be peace

# The Leader

HALALCO

HALALCO BOOKS

Halalco Books
155 Hillwood Avenue
Falls Church, VA 22046



Library of Congress Cataloging in Publishing Data.

The Prophets' Stories for Children,
Set of 21 volumes

ISBN: 978-1-881963-462

Vol. 14, Harun - The Leader

First Edition: September 1993
Al-Saadawi Publications

Second Printing: April 2012
Halalco Books

ISBN: 978-1-881963-318

Halalco Books

# HARUN
## upon whom be peace
# The Leader

**By**
**Amina Ibrahim Ali**

Edited by
**J. C. Cinquino**
**Ayesha DeLorenzo**

Illustrated by
**Ayesha DeLorenzo**

HALALCO
HALALCO BOOKS
155 Hillwood Avenue
Falls Church, VA 22046
Phone: 703-532-3202
Fax: 703-543-3212
halalco@halalco.com

## References


THE HOLY QURAN

THE PROPHETS' STORIES, in Arabic, by Ibn Kathir

THE PROPHETS' STORIES, in Arabic, by Al Najar

PROPHETHOOD AND THE PROPHETS, in Arabic, by Muhammad Ali Al Sabouni

THE BIOGRAPHIES OF THE PROPHETS OF GOD AS MENTIONED IN THE GLORIOUS QURAN, in English, by Samih Atef El Zein

The Prophet Harun (peace be upon him) was born one year before his brother, the Prophet Musa, in the year before the Pharaoh ordered all Israelite boy children put to the sword.

When Almighty Allah gave Musa (peace be upon him) his mission in the sacred valley of Tuwa, Musa's first request was for his brother Harun to help him.

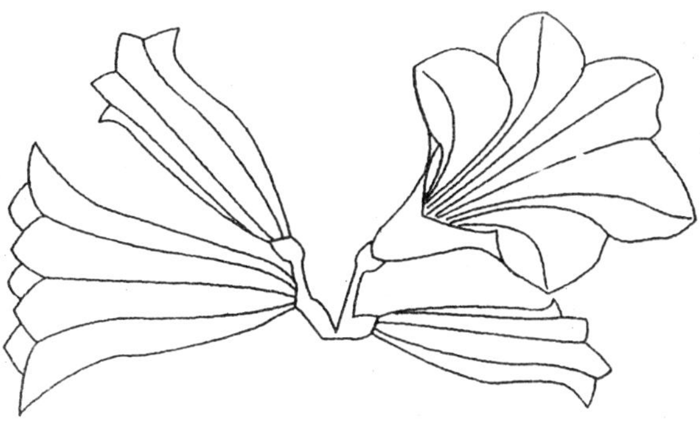

He said, "Harun, my brother, is more eloquent than I am. Let him assist me, O Allah."

Almighty Allah replied, "We will strengthen your arm with your brother and give you both such authority that they will not be able to harm you. By showing them Our signs, you and your followers will be victorious."

So Musa and Harun (peace be upon them) were appoint prophets by Allah at the same time. Harun remained

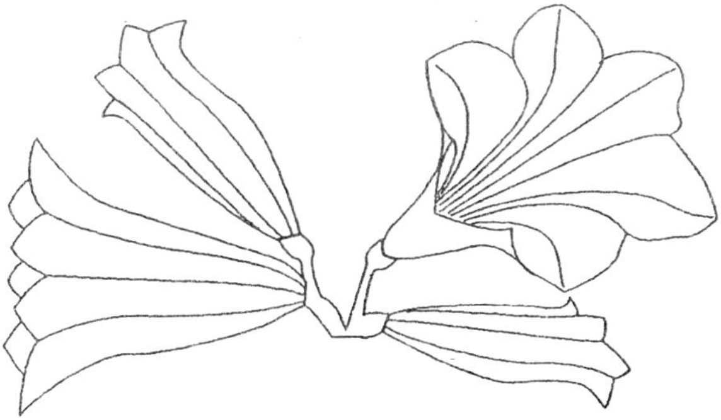

steadfast at his brother's side, helping him and reinforcing his message. Their mission was a very difficult one. They were to go to the Pharaoh and call him to the true religion. By speaking the truth to him and showing him Allah's miraculous signs, they were to convince him that there was one God, Allah, and that all creation in the heavens and earth belonged to Him.

Then, if people worshipped Allah and obeyed his law, they would be

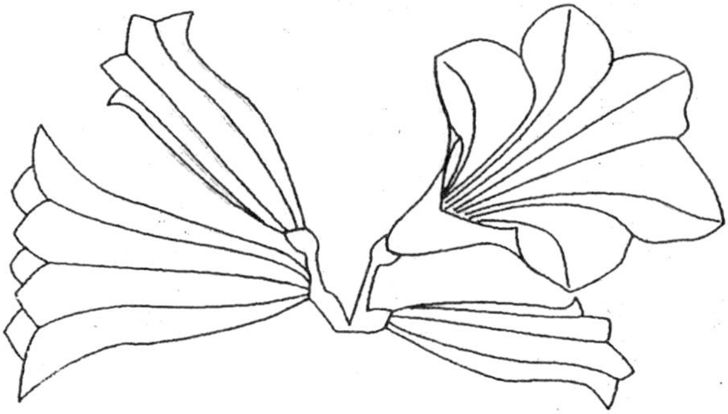

rewarded. But if they rejected Him and lived their lives as they pleased, they would be punished.

One of those who rejected Allah and His signs was the haughty Israelite, Qarun. But Allah destroyed Qarun and those who followed him by swallowing them up in the earth. Both Harun and Musa felt that when the Pharaoh saw what had happened to Qarun, he might decide to change his ways. So they attempted again to bring the Pharaoh to the true religion. Instead

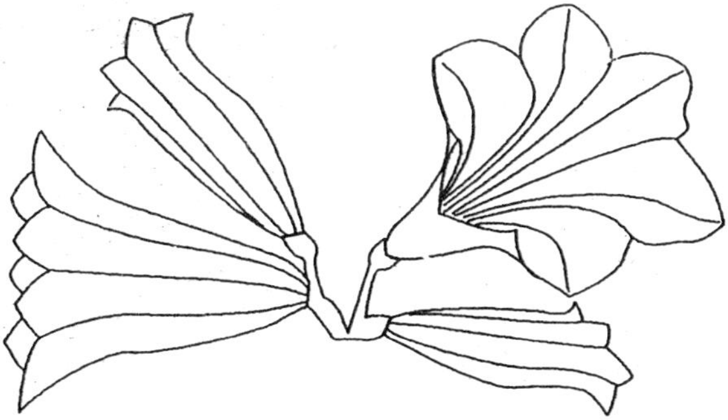

of accepting the truth, however, the Pharaoh ridiculed Allah's prophet about the simple woolen clothes they wore.

"Are you not surprised at these poor humble men?" the Pharaoh said, "They think they are in charge of making my power permanent and my kingdom safe! Shall I throw a golden bracelet on them to show that I revere gold and hate wool?"

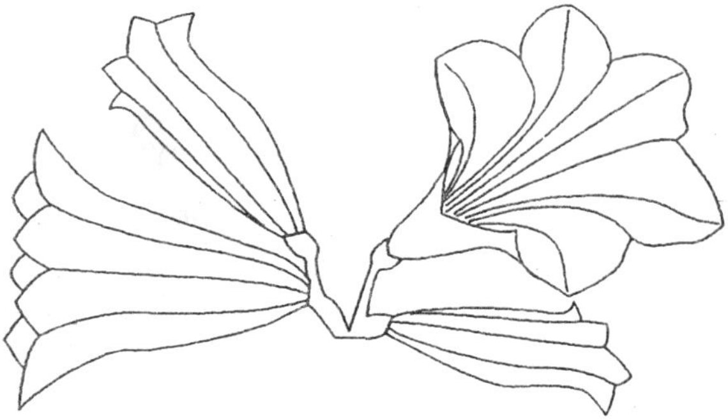

Thus, the Pharaoh rejected the message the two prophets brought to him. Finally, he was destroyed with his army when the seas that had parted for Musa and the believers crashed back and drowned them.

When Almighty Allah summoned Musa to Mount Sinai, Musa entrusted the responsibility of the people to Harun.

"Act for me amongst my people," Musa said to his brother. "Do right,

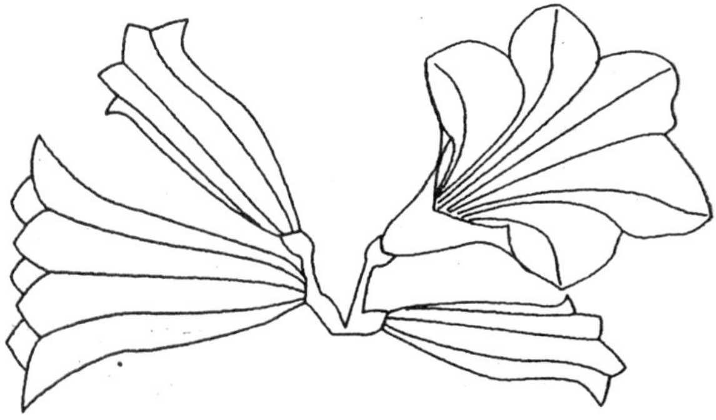

and folow not the way of those who do mischief."

Musa went up to the mountain. When thirty days had gone by, Almighty Allah commanded that Musa stay for ten more days. But the people down in the desert below expected Musa after thirty days. When he did not return they wondered as to the reason why.

Among them were doubters and the weak of faith. When Musa failed to

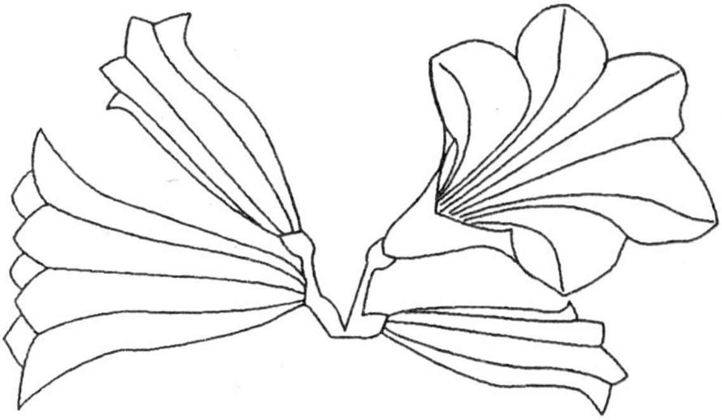

appear on the appointed day, they began to ridicule him and his mission to the mountain. Rumors spread among the people, and there was much talking. Some people said that Musa had abandoned them, and that he had broken his promise to them to return and lead them from the barren and sandy desert to a land of rivers and green pastures.

Amidst all the rumors and talk of broken promises, Harun did his best to convince the believers to keep their

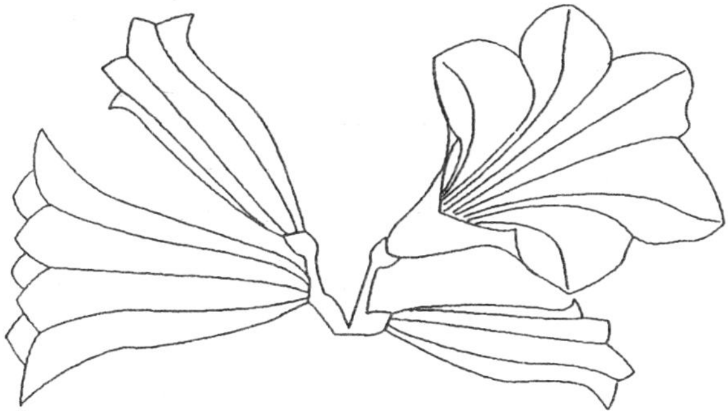

faith in Musa and the message he brought to them from Allah.

But many people listened instead to those who spread the rumors, and they lost faith. "After all," they said to one another, "if Musa has not kept his promise to us, then why should we keep our promise to him?"

Among the faithless people was a man called Al Samiri. When he saw how effective the rumors had been in confusing the people and causing them

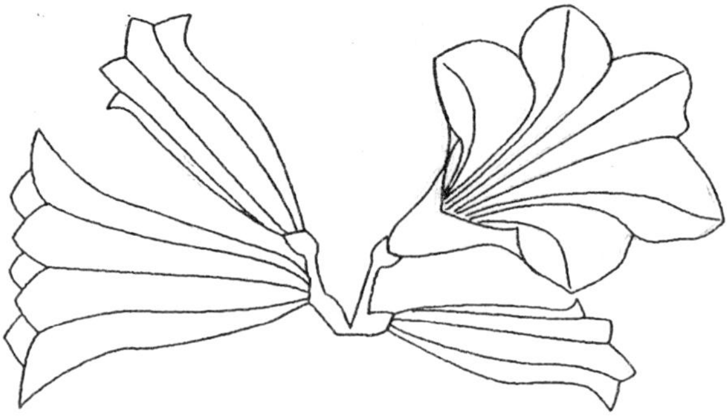

to doubt, he realised that he had a chance to take over as the people's new leader.

Al Samiri told the people that if they gave him their golden ornaments and jewelry, he would create a new god for them to worship. With the gold he collected from the faithless people, Al Samiri fashioned a golden calf.

When the wind blew through the golden calf, it caused an echo that sounded very much like the lowing of

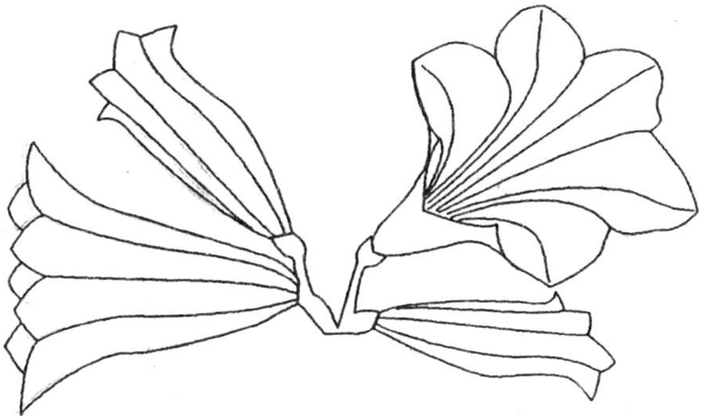

a real cow. Throughout several dark nights, the people listened to the haunting sound of the wind echoing through the calf. Al Samiri told them that the calf was a god and that they should worship it. Finally, most of the people were convinced that what he said was true, and they began worshipping the calf.

Harun told the people that Al Samiri was deceiving them, and that the calf was no more than a statue. "Only Allah is your god, and only He is

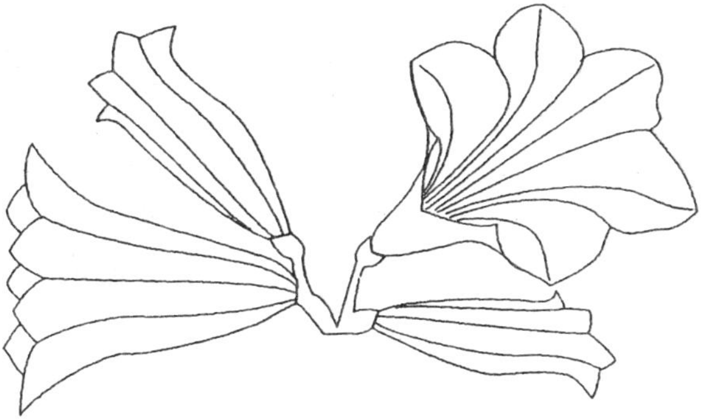

deserving of worship," Harun told the people. "Al Samiri is making fools of you. Allah is your god, and Musa is His Messenger."

But only a few of them believed Harun. The rest of the people laughed at him. "Where's Musa?" they would ask him. "And where is Musa's Allah?"

Then they would point toward the golden calf and say, "There is our god. Our god is golden, and we can hear it

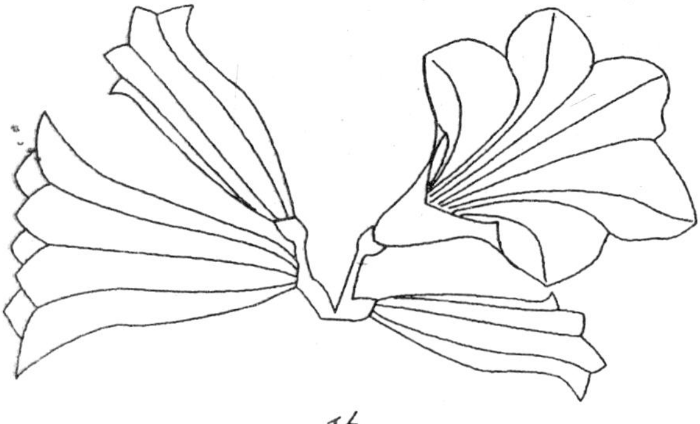

speak! What can your god do? We have never seen the god of Musa, and we have never heard him. But our god is real, and it will make us powerful."

At first, Harun and the believers thought that they should fight against Al Samiri and his followers. But before they could, the people tried to kill Harun. After that, Harun understood that fighting was not the best way to make the people believe in the truth. Instead, Harun and his followers

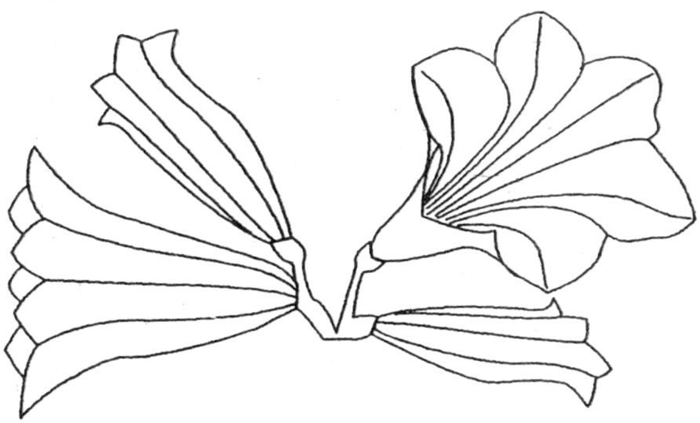

attempted to show the people the right way by speaking to them about Allah and the true religion.

At long last, one day Musa came down from the mountain. But when he saw the calf and the people worshipping it, he became very angry. When he met Harun, Musa grasped him by his beard and said, "O Harun! Why didn't you do something when you saw them go astray? Did you decide to disobey me too?"

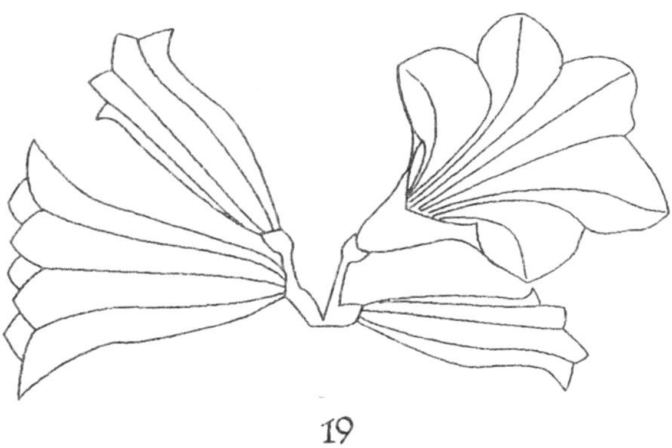

Harun replied, "O son of my mother! I tried to stop them, but they would not listen to me. Instead, they tried to kill me. Please do not let our enemies rejoice over my misfortune, and do not suppose me to be a sinner."

Musa was relieved to know that his brother had not disobeyed him. Musa said a prayer to Allah, "O Allah! Forgive me and my brother! Grant us Your mercy! You are the most merciful of those who show mercy!"

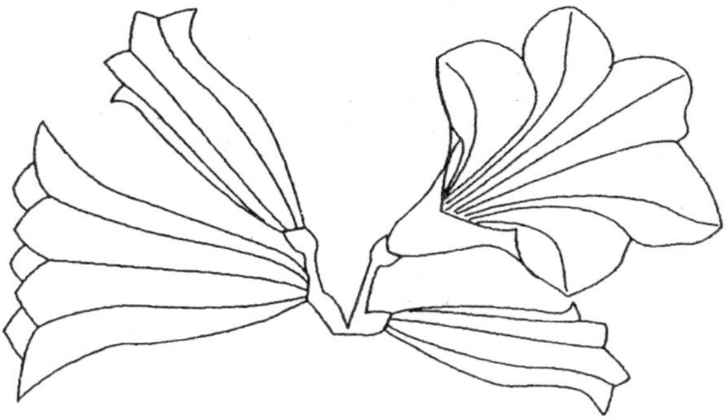

Musa knew that his brother was not guilty of any wrongdoing. Even so, he prayed for forgiveness for himself and for his brother. He prayed for forgiveness for himself because he had been so angry with Harun; and he prayed for forgiveness for Harun because he had been unable to control the people.

Musa and Harun knew that many of their people were weak in faith, and that those whose faith was strong were few.

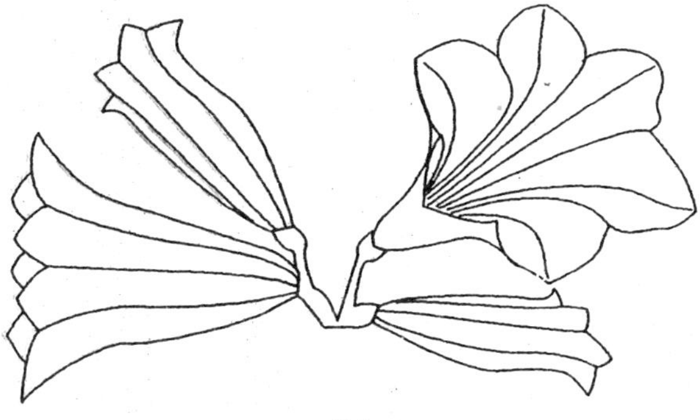

A time came when they reached the land of Kanan, on the other side of the great Sinai desert. But when the time came to begin settling there, Musa's people became afraid. They had lived as slaves under the Pharaoh in Egypt for so long that the idea of living on their own was frightening to them. To them, the hardships of the desert were better than beginning a new life in a new land. And so they began to tell each other stories about the giants and terrible things they would find in Kanan. Even though Musa and

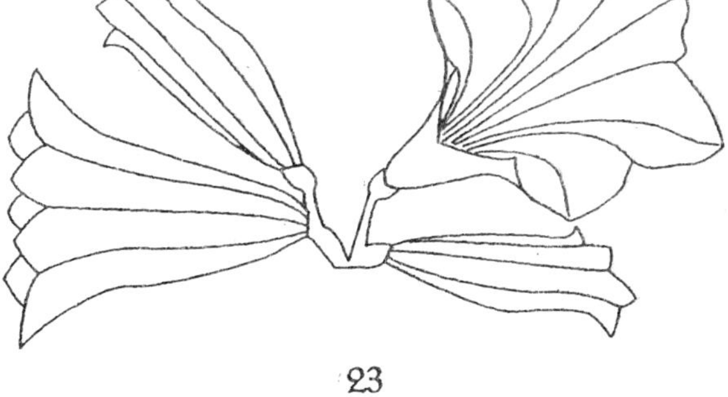

Harun did their best to urge their people to leave the desert, their efforts came to nothing. Finally, Musa realised that the only person who supported him was his brother, Harun. Musa prayed to Allah, "O Lord! I have control only over myself and my brother. Do not count us among these rebellious people!"

Allah commanded Musa to leave his brother in charge of the people, and to wander in solitude for forty years. When Musa returned, he found that

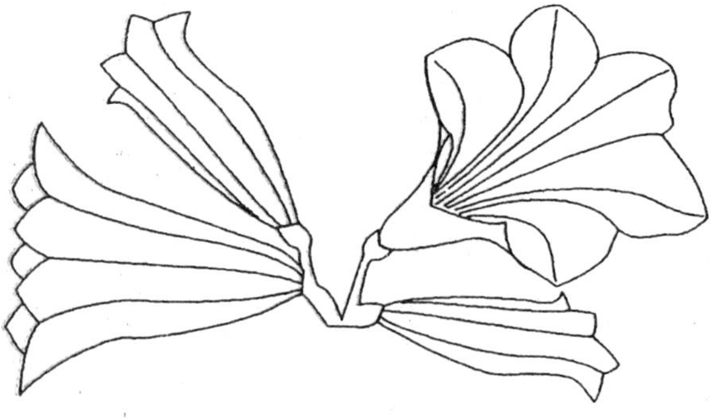

his brother had died just before his arrival. A year later, Musa himself died. Both prophets died in the desert, caring for the people they had delivered from oppression.

In all the years they had spent in the desert, a new generation had grown up. These were people who had never known slavery, and who had learned to endure the hardships of life in the wilderness. Moreover, they were a believing people who had matured under the teachings of Harun about

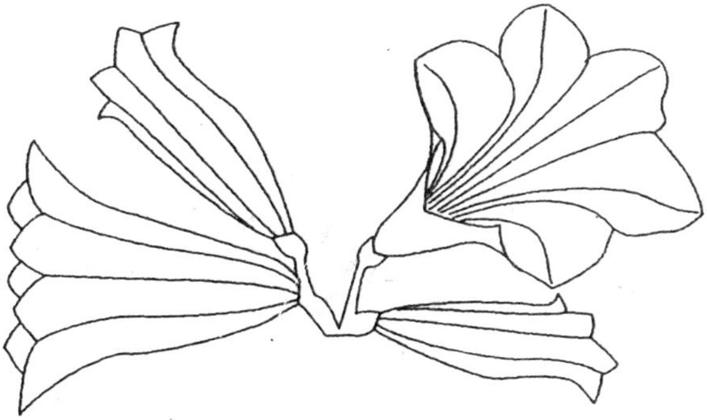

Almighty Allah, and their faith made them strong. Stories of giants in Kanan would not deter them from leaving the desert and making a better life for themselves and their children.

Finally, the vision held by Musa and Harun came true. The new generation of believers left the desert to settle in the land of Kanan.

"Peace and salutations to Musa and Harun! This is the way We reward those who do right."

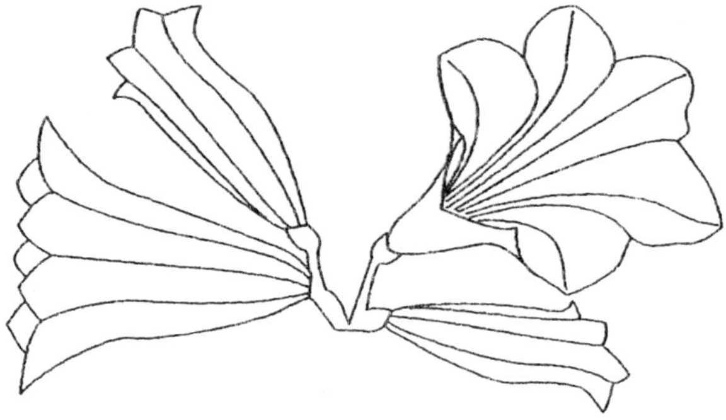

# GLOSSARY

AI SAMIRI... a wicked man who made the golden calf

MUSA... one of Allah's Prophets, and Harun's brother

PHAROAH... the powerful king of Egypt

QARUN... a haughty Israelite

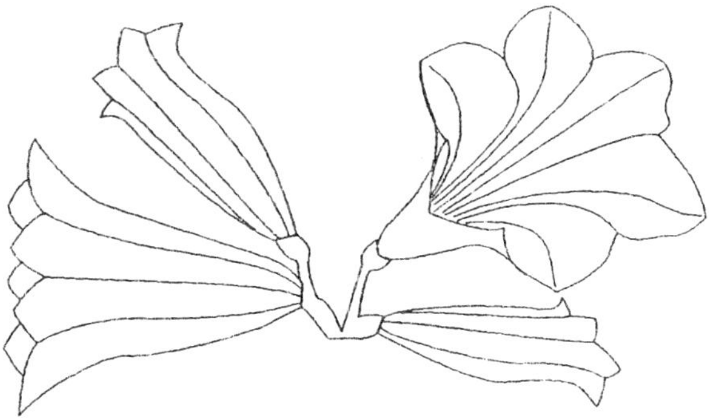

Printed in India